SWEET and SOUR

Far from Ordinary Fruity Desserts

by HEATHER KIM

COMPASS POINT BOOKS
a capstone imprint

Pear Cheesecake with
Ginger Gastrique **20**

Baked Apple Brie Croûte **34**

Berry Paletas **44**

TABLE OF CONTENTS

BETTER WITH FRUIT

Do you love making your own desserts? Or maybe you just love eating them, especially desserts that add the sweet and sour goodness of fruit? Take your desserts to the next level with these new and improved twists on traditional recipes. Whether you're craving sweet flavors of berries or pears, or the tangy, tart tastes of lemons or cranberries, you're sure to find something to tickle your taste buds.

From lemony, ginger molasses cookies to sour grape panna cotta, these scrumptious recipes are sure to please any sweet tooth. Grab your apron, follow the safety tips and tricks, and you'll soon see dessert-making is a piece of cake!

PLAYING IT SAFE

Measuring precisely and following the directions should yield great results and fine desserts. Don't ruin your success by having an accident in the kitchen. Follow these safety precautions as you work:

Always wash your hands before you begin baking, if you spill, and after touching raw eggs.

Use caution when handling sharp objects. Ask for an adult's help when a recipe calls for chopping, slicing, or cutting. Hold the knife's handle firmly when cutting and keep fingers away from the blade.

Also be careful when working near hot surfaces. It's best to have an adult help when operating the stovetop and oven at high temperatures. When using saucepans, turn the handles toward the center of the stove to avoid bumping a handle and spilling. Always wear oven mitts or pot holders to take hot baking sheets or cake pans out of the oven.

Spills and messes are bound to take place in the kitchen. Wipe up messes with paper towels or a damp kitchen towel. Keep your countertop clean and dry.

MIX IT UP

Before you gather up supplies and go shopping for ingredients, read through each recipe. Some recipes require waiting several hours or overnight for food to prepare. Make sure you plan accordingly.

Also make sure you know how to perform each technique. Here are a few common baking procedures you may need to perform.

mixing bowl

electric mixer

food processor

mixing spoon

6

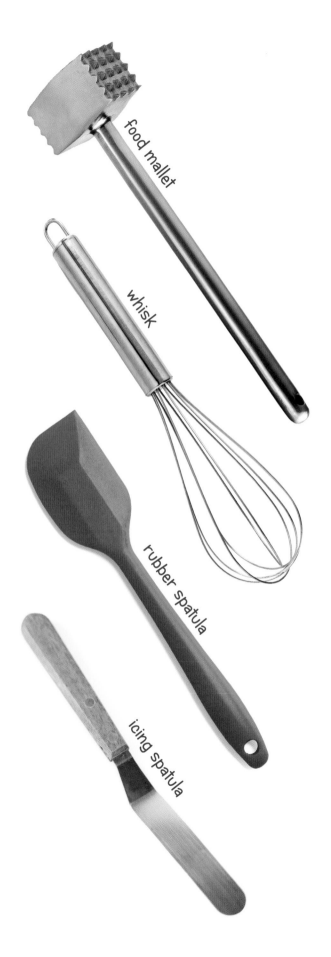

food mallet

whisk

rubber spatula

icing spatula

BEAT IT
Create a smooth, creamy mixture by stirring briskly, using a spoon, whisk, or mixer.

CREAM IT
Vigorously beat and stir ingredients. The result? Creamy, fluffy smoothness.

DIVIDE IT
If an ingredient is "divided" or "separated," you'll only use part of the total amount at one time.

WHIP IT
Add air and volume to a mixture using a whisk or mixer.

WHISK IT
Use a whisk to combine ingredients using a side-to-side motion. If you don't have a whisk, use two forks.

ZEST IT
Shred tiny bits of the outer, colorful rind or peel of a citrus fruit to add fresh flavor to the recipe.

NOT YOUR GRANDMA'S COOKIES

Move over, chocolate chips! Make room for tangy, zesty fruit-filled cookies. These sweet and sour recipes will satisfy all your cravings. They taste so good, you'll want to share them with everyone you know.

MOLASSES GINGERSNAPS WITH LEMON CURD

Without the sour, life just isn't as sweet. Sandwich some lemon curd between two gingersnaps for a tangy yet sugary surprise.

GINGERSNAPS

2 cups all-purpose flour

2 teaspoons baking soda

1/2 teaspoon salt

1 tablespoon dried ginger powder

1 teaspoon cinnamon

3/4 cup vegetable shortening

1 cup granulated sugar

1 egg

1/4 cup dark molasses

1/3 cup Sugar in the Raw®

1 Preheat oven to 350°F.

2 In a medium bowl, whisk all the dry ingredients together and set aside.

3 In a larger mixing bowl, mix vegetable shortening and granulated sugar together until fluffy. Add the egg, molasses, and dry ingredients, and mix together.

4 Shape dough into 1-inch (2.5-cm) balls, roll in the Sugar in the Raw®, and place 2 inches (5 cm) apart on an ungreased baking sheet.

5 Bake for about 7 minutes. Turn the sheet and bake another 5 minutes or so.

6 Remove them from the oven when the edges are firm and the centers are soft. Cool on the sheet for 1 minute. Then move to a rack and let cool completely.

Recipe continues on next page.

– SASSY TIP –
No cooling rack? No worries. Let the cookies sit on the pan for a couple minutes. Then flip them upside down on the same sheet.

11

LEMON CURD

1/2 cup lemon juice

1/2 cup granulated sugar

2 large egg yolks

2 large eggs

1/2 teaspoon salt

6 tablespoons butter

1 Place a fine mesh strainer over a medium bowl and set aside.

2 In another bowl, whisk together the lemon juice, sugar, egg yolks, eggs, and salt. Set aside.

3 Melt butter in a medium saucepan over low heat. Turn heat to medium and add the lemon juice mixture, whisking until it thickens into a pudding.

4 Take off heat and smash through the mesh strainer. Refrigerate until cooled.

TO ASSEMBLE

Dunk plain cookies directly into a bowlful of the curd, or sandwich the curd between two cookies.

– SASSY TIP –

To separate egg yolks from the whites, crack open the egg. Let the whites fall into a bowl below. Move the yolk back and forth between the two halves of the cracked egg until all the white has fallen below. Save the whites for another use. Remember to always wash your hands with soap and water after touching raw eggs.

SOFT GINGER MOLASSES COOKIES WITH LEMON ICING

COOKIES

3/4 cup coconut oil

1 cup granulated sugar

1 egg, beaten

1/4 cup dark molasses

2 cups all-purpose flour

2 teaspoons baking soda

1/2 teaspoon salt

1 tablespoon ginger

1 teaspoon cinnamon

1/3 cup demerara sugar

1 **Preheat oven to 350°F.**

2 **In a large bowl, mix coconut oil and sugar until creamy.**

3 **Add the egg and then the molasses. Add the remaining ingredients (except the demerara sugar) and mix until well-combined.**

4 **Shape dough into 1-inch (2.5-cm) balls and roll them in the demerara sugar.**

5 **Bake on an ungreased baking sheet for about 10 minutes or until cookies are set.**

ICING

4 cups powdered sugar

3 tablespoons lemon juice (tweak for preferred smoothness)

pinch of salt

1 **In a medium to large bowl, stir the ingredients until smooth.**

2 **Spread icing onto cookies with a butter knife or spoon.**

SASSY FACT
Demerara sugar is a raw, large-grained, golden-amber sugar. It has a more caramel-like taste than regular brown sugar.

FIGGY COOKIES

These cookies are light, flaky, and oh-so-delicious—not to mention easy to make. Spread store-bought jam in between two layers of dough and bake. If you can't find fig jam, try another fruity flavor!

DOUGH

1 cup granulated sugar

1/2 cup butter, room temperature

1 large egg

1 tablespoon heavy cream

1/2 teaspoon vanilla extract

1/2 teaspoon salt

1 teaspoon baking powder

1 3/4 cups all-purpose flour

FILLING

10- or 12-ounce jar fig jam

1 For the dough, whisk together the sugar, butter, egg, heavy cream, and vanilla extract until well-blended. Add the dry ingredients and mix well.

2 Refrigerate for about an hour.

3 Preheat oven to 350°F.

4 Split the dough in half. Roll out both dough halves to about 0.25-inch (0.6-cm) thickness.

5 Line a 13- x 9-inch (33- x 23-cm) baking dish with the first half of dough. Using a butter knife or spatula, evenly spread fig jam on top. Cover the jam with the second half of the dough.

6 Bake for about 30 minutes, turning once halfway through.

7 Let cool completely. Cut into squares or preferred shapes.

EVERYTHING BUT THE BIRTHDAY CAKE

Cakes are not just for birthdays! Bake one of these fruity cakes anytime you want. Do you prefer citrusy-sweet or sour-as-grapes? Whatever you're craving, these bold cakes will please your taste buds.

PEAR CHEESECAKE WITH GINGER GASTRIQUE

With a creamy filling and a crumbly crust, it's no surprise that cheesecake has been a favorite dessert for decades. Top with poached pears and ginger gastrique for a daring twist.

CHEESECAKE

**3/4 cup granulated sugar +
2 tablespoons for coating**

**16 ounces cream cheese,
softened to room
temperature**

**12 ounces chèvre, room
temperature**

1 tablespoon lemon juice

1 tablespoon vanilla extract

1/2 teaspoon salt

1 cup sour cream

6 eggs, room temperature

> **– SASSY TIP –**
> If your ingredients are NOT
> at room temperature. the mix
> will seize and be lumpy.

1 **Preheat oven to
350°F.**

2 **In a large mixing bowl,
whip together the sugar,
cream cheese, and chèvre
until silky and smooth.
Then add remaining
ingredients and mix until
even silkier and smoother.**

3 **Pour the batter into a
9-inch (23-cm) springform
pan.**

4 **Place the springform
pan into a cake pan or
roasting pan and fill
with very hot water.
Bake in the water bath
until completely set and
slightly golden, about
50 to 60 minutes.**

POACHED PEARS

1 quart water

1 1/3 cups granulated sugar

**4 pears, peeled, cored, and
quartered**

Optional:

cinnamon stick

whole cloves

black peppercorns

fresh lemon

vanilla extract

star anise

fresh ginger slices

1 **In a large saucepan over
medium heat, add the water
and sugar, stirring until
dissolved. Add optional
ingredients, if desired.**

2 **Add the pears and simmer
15 to 25 minutes, or until
pears can be sliced with a
butter knife.**

3 **Remove from heat and let
cool in their liquid.**

Recipe continues on next page. →

> **SASSY FACT**
> The water bath allows the
> cheesecake to bake more evenly.
> It also keeps the oven moist and
> helps prevent the cheesecake
> from drying out and cracking.

GINGER GASTRIQUE

1/2 cup minced fresh ginger

3/4 cup apple cider vinegar

1 cup sugar

1 In a small saucepan, bring the ginger and apple cider vinegar to a boil.

2 Stir in the sugar. Lower the heat and simmer for 20 minutes.

3 Strain and let cool completely.

GINGERSNAP SAND

8 ounces gingersnaps

2 tablespoons butter, melted

1/4 cup granulated sugar

2 teaspoons salt

1 Using a food processor, grind gingersnaps until crumbly. If you don't have a food processor, break up with your hands. You can also put in a sealed baggie and smash with a meat tenderizer.

2 In a medium bowl, mix together the crumbled gingersnaps, butter, sugar, and salt, until fully combined.

TO ASSEMBLE:

1 On a large plate or serving platter, layer gingersnap sand, cheesecake, and pears.

2 Drizzle with ginger gastrique.

3 Slice and serve.

ELVIS BANANA CUPCAKES

Need a new banana-flavored dessert? Try these "Big Hunk O' Love" Elvis Banana Cupcakes topped with peanut buttercream frosting and butterscotch candied bacon. The sweet and salty combo will melt in your mouth!

Thank you. Thank you very much.

CUPCAKES

1 2/3 cups all-purpose flour

1/2 teaspoon salt

1 teaspoon baking soda

1/4 teaspoon baking powder

1 cup granulated sugar

1/3 cup butter, softened

2 eggs

3 or 4 medium bananas, ripened and mashed

1/3 cup water

1/2 teaspoon vanilla extract

1 Preheat oven to 350°F. Butter or spray two muffin pans and line with cupcake papers.

2 In a medium bowl, mix together the flour, salt, baking soda, and baking powder. Set aside.

3 In a large bowl, mix together the sugar and butter until light and fluffy. Add the eggs, bananas, water, and vanilla extract, and combine.

4 Mix in the dry ingredients until just moist.

5 Bake for 1 hour, turning once.

PEANUT BUTTERCREAM FROSTING

1/2 cup butter, softened

1 cup creamy peanut butter

2 cups powdered sugar

3 tablespoons milk, as needed

1 In a medium mixing bowl, beat butter and peanut butter together with an electric mixer.

2 Slowly add the sugar. When mixture starts to thicken, after about 3 minutes, add milk, one tablespoon at a time, until frosting is spreadable.

Recipe continues on next page.

BUTTERSCOTCH CANDIED BACON

8 ounces bacon

8 to 10 hard butterscotch candies

1 Cook bacon according to package instructions until crispy. Drain and pat with paper towel to absorb grease. Place cooked bacon on rimmed baking sheet. Set aside.

2 In a nonstick pan over low heat, **CAREFULLY** melt down butterscotch candies. Immediately pour over the bacon, spreading evenly.

3 Let cool completely. Then break candied bacon into bite-sized pieces.

TO ASSEMBLE

1 Using an icing spatula or butter knife, frost banana bread muffins with peanut buttercream frosting.

2 Top frosted muffins with butterscotch candied bacon.

– SASSY TIP –
If you want to make this dessert even more daring, garnish with baby pickles.

CRANBERRY ORANGE PECAN CAKE

A fluffy cranberry-filled cake topped with a lemony, toasted pecan glaze and a hint of orange zest—what's not to love? This moist, tart, and delicious dessert is perfect for anyone who loves a nutty addition to their treats!

CAKE

2 tablespoons + 1 1/4 cups granulated sugar

1 1/2 cups cranberries (fresh or dried)

2 teaspoons baking powder

1 1/2 cups all-purpose flour

1 cup powdered sugar

1/2 teaspoon salt

1/2 cup butter, melted

3 large eggs

1 orange, zested and juiced

1 teaspoon vanilla extract

1 cup sour cream

1 Preheat oven to 350°F. Line a Bundt cake mold with butter and dust with flour.

2 Sprinkle 2 tablespoons of sugar and then 1/4 cup of the cranberries on the bottom of the pan. Set aside.

3 In a medium bowl, whisk together the baking powder, powdered sugar, and salt. Add the remaining cranberries.

4 In a separate mixing bowl, cream together butter and the remaining granulated sugar until pale-yellow and fluffy. Scrape down sides. Crack in eggs, one by one, and then mix until well-combined. Add orange juice and zest, vanilla extract, and sour cream.

5 Fold the dry ingredients into wet mixture. Stir until just combined.

6 Pour into the prepared pan and bake 45 minutes or until a toothpick comes out clean.

7 Remove cake from oven and allow to rest for 15 minutes. Then flip cake onto a wire rack to cool.

GLAZE

1 1/4 cups powdered sugar

pinch of salt

2 teaspoons lemon juice

1 to 2 tablespoons whole milk

1/4 cup dried cranberries, chopped

1/2 cup toasted pecans, chopped

orange zest, to sprinkle

1 In a medium bowl, mix the powdered sugar, salt, juice, and milk until completely combined.

2 Drizzle the glaze over cooled cake. Sprinkle with cranberries, pecans, and orange zest.

PLEASE PASS THE PASTRIES

Pastries can be a dessert, a snack, or an appetizer. Whenever and however you have them, these pastries will look and taste amazing.

RHUBARB TURNOVERS WITH RHUBARB COMPOTE AND GASTRIQUE

Shhh! This recipe has a secret. Rhubarb is technically a vegetable. It grows stalks similar to celery. It's too tart to eat raw, so it must be cooked. Make these turnovers in the spring, when rhubarb is in season.

COMPOTE

4 cups rhubarb, diced

1 cup sugar

pinch of salt

– SASSY TIP – Do not eat the leaves of rhubarb. They are poisonous and can make you sick.

1 In a small saucepan, stir rhubarb and sugar together. Let sit for about 10 minutes or until water leaches out of the rhubarb.

2 Cook on low for 15 minutes, keeping rhubarb bright and textured.

3 Drain rhubarb into containers. Save the liquid for the gastrique.

RHUBARB GASTRIQUE

4 parts rhubarb liquid

2 parts sugar

1 part apple cider vinegar

TO MAKE

In a small saucepan, warm gently on low until sugar is completely dissolved. Set aside.

TURNOVER

1 package puff pastry, cut into squares

1 egg, whisked

Sugar in the Raw®, for sprinkling

1 Preheat oven to 350°F.

2 Place puff pastry square on a Silpat®- or parchment-lined baking sheet.

3 Spoon rhubarb compote into the center of each square.

4 Fold squares over into triangles. Seal the edges by crimping with a fork or pinching them together.

5 Lightly brush the entire top of the turnovers with whisked egg. Sprinkle with Sugar in the Raw®.

6 Bake until puffy, flaky, and golden-brown. Drizzle with gastrique.

SASSY FACT
Made for nonstick cooking, a Silpat® silicone rubber mat is great when working with sticky stuff, like gooey batter, taffy, caramel, or dough.

BAKED APPLE BRIE CROÛTE

This simple baked Brie recipe is filled with ooey-gooey cheese. all wrapped in a perfectly puffed pastry. Brie is a soft. mild creamy cheese from France. Munch on this with tart and tangy apples for an easy (but yummy!) dessert or appetizer.

INGREDIENTS

16 ounces Brie (wheel or wedge)

1 puff pastry sheet, thawed

1 egg yolk

apple slices

1 Preheat oven to 400°F. Line a sheet pan with parchment paper.

2 Unfold puff pastry and wrap around Brie—folding, stretching, and smoothing, until cheese is completely covered.

3 Place Brie, seam-side down, on the papered pan. Brush egg yolk over the entire dome.

4 Bake for 30 minutes or until golden-brown. Let stand for about 45 minutes.

5 Eat warm with tart apples.

– SASSY TIP –
Choose apples that will pair best with the richness of the Brie. Crispy apples, such as Granny Smith, Haralson, or Honeycrisp, work best.

NO OVEN NEEDED

What is better than homemade dessert? How about homemade dessert that doesn't need to be baked! These sweet recipes are as simple as they come—no oven required. Bon appétit!

SOUR GRAPE PANNA COTTA

Panna cotta means "cooked cream" in Italian. It's a rich. pudding-like dessert. This panna cotta is topped with a grape-elicious gelatin to make for a creamy. fruity treat.

SOUR GRAPE GELATIN

1 teaspoon unflavored gelatin

1 cup grape juice, separated

1 tablespoon fresh lemon juice

1 cup red or green seedless grapes, thinly sliced

PANNA COTTA

1 envelope unflavored gelatin (about 1 tablespoon)

2 tablespoons cold water

2 cups heavy cream

1 cup half-and-half

1/3 cup sugar

1 1/2 teaspoons vanilla extract

1 Start by making the sour grape gelatin. In a small saucepan, sprinkle the gelatin over 1/4 cup grape juice until it softens, about 5 minutes.

2 Bring gelatin to a simmer, stirring until dissolved. Remove from the flame and stir in the remaining 3/4 cup grape juice, lemon juice, and grape slices.

3 Line six ramekins with nonstick cooking oil or spray. Divide the grape mixture among ramekins. Freeze until set, about 30 minutes.

4 Meanwhile, make the panna cotta. In a small saucepan, mix gelatin in the water until it is softened. Stir over low heat until gelatin is dissolved. Set aside.

5 In a large saucepan, stir the cream, half-and-half, and sugar. Bring to a boil. Remove pan from heat. Stir in gelatin mixture and vanilla extract. Strain.

6 Divide cream mixture among each ramekin. Cover with plastic wrap. Refrigerate at least 4 hours, up to overnight.

TO SERVE

Dip ramekins, one at a time, into a bowl of hot water for about 3 seconds. Run a thin knife around the edge of each ramekin to loosen. Flip onto a serving dish.

> **– SASSY TIP –**
> Ramekins are small, ceramic bowls, perfect for baking individual desserts. For this recipe, if you don't have ramekins, a silicone muffin tray or an ice tray works in a pinch.

39

COEUR À LA CRÈME

In French *coeur à la crème* means "heart with cream." Traditionally the dessert is molded into a heart shape. Whichever way you shape it, this dessert is creamy, refreshing, and delicious.

INGREDIENTS

4 10- x 10-inch (25- x 25-cm) squares cheesecloth

8-ounce package cream cheese, room temperature

1 cup sour cream

6 tablespoons powdered sugar, divided

1 teaspoon lemon juice (preferably fresh)

1/2 teaspoon vanilla extract

pinch of salt

2 cups fresh fruit

1 Dampen the cheesecloth with water and line four coeur à la crème molds with a square of cheesecloth each. If you don't have coeur à la crème molds, line a colander with cheesecloth and set inside of a bowl.

2 In a large mixing bowl, whip the cream cheese, sour cream, 4 tablespoons powdered sugar, lemon juice, vanilla extract, and salt until smooth, about 4 minutes.

3 Strain the mixture and divide among the molds or pour into colander. Fold cheesecloth over and cover with plastic wrap.

4 Refrigerate for 2 hours to overnight.

TO ASSEMBLE

1 Unwrap the molds and flip them onto plates. If using a colander, remove and cut into four pieces.

2 Top with fresh fruit and sprinkle with powdered sugar.

ETON MESS

Desserts don't have to look pretty to taste good. This refreshing, easy-to-assemble dessert gets the first part of its name from Eton College in England, where it is believed to have originated. The second part needs no explanation.

INGREDIENTS

4 cups fresh strawberries

2 cups whipping cream

2 teaspoons sugar

1/2 teaspoon vanilla extract

pinch of salt

1 package meringues

1 Chop up the berries. Set aside.

2 Using an electric mixer, whip the cream and sugar on high speed until fluffy and peaking.

3 Stir in vanilla extract and salt until completely combined.

TO ASSEMBLE

Top meringues with whipped cream and strawberries, alternating layers.

MAKE YOUR OWN MERINGUES

1 1/2 tablespoons cornstarch

1 1/2 cups granulated sugar

6 egg whites (see page 13)

1/3 teaspoon cream of tartar

pinch of salt

1 1/2 teaspoons vanilla extract

1 Preheat oven to 275°F. Line a sheet pan with parchment paper or Silpat® mat.

2 In a small bowl, whisk the cornstarch and sugar. Set aside.

3 In a large mixing bowl, whip the egg whites, cream of tartar, and salt on medium for about 2 to 3 minutes or until a froth forms.

4 Mix in the cornstarch and sugar and whip until fluffy. When stiff, glossy peaks form, add the vanilla extract.

5 With a large spoon, create little bird nest-like shapes onto the prepped sheet pan.

6 Bake for 20 to 30 minutes and turn. Repeat until meringues are dry and bottoms are pale yellow.

– SASSY TIP –
If you're using subpar strawberries, or berries out of season, add a little fresh lemon juice and sugar until deliciousness ensues.

BERRY PALETAS

Serve these berry paletas at your next outdoor picnic or backyard party. Filled with juicy berries of your choosing, orange juice, and a tinge of lemon, these sweet, berry-licious pops are a cool treat on a hot day.

INGREDIENTS

4 cups your favorite fresh berries

1 cup granulated sugar

1/2 cup orange juice

pinch of salt

2 tablespoons lemon juice

1 **Stir berries and sugar together in a medium saucepan. Let rest for about 15 minutes. Add orange juice and salt.**

2 **Bring to a boil, reduce heat, and simmer for 5 minutes. Remove from heat. Let cool to room temperature.**

3 **Pour mixture along with the lemon juice into a blender. Blend until combined.**

4 **Divide evenly among ice pop molds. Cover molds with the lid. Add the ice pop sticks.**

5 **Freeze for about 5 hours or until completely frozen.**

– SASSY TIP –

No ice pop molds? Make your own! Find small, food-safe containers, such as tiny disposable cups or large ice-cube molds. Cut a piece of sturdy construction paper or cardboard to fit over it. Poke a hole in the center large enough for an ice pop stick and voilà!

METRIC CONVERSIONS

The measurements used in this book are
imperial units. If you use metric units, look here.

TEMPERATURE

275°F	135°C
350°F	180°C

VOLUME

1/4 teaspoon	1.25 grams or milliliters
1/3 teaspoon	1.5 g or 1.5 mL
1/2 teaspoon	2.5 g or mL
1 teaspoon	5 g or mL
1 tablespoon	15 g or mL
1/4 cup	57 g (dry) or 60 mL (liquid)
1/3 cup	75 g (dry) or 80 mL (liquid)
1/2 cup	114 g (dry) or 125 mL (liquid)
2/3 cup	150 g (dry) or 160 mL (liquid)
3/4 cup	170 g (dry) or 175 mL (liquid)
1 cup	227 g (dry) or 240 mL (liquid)
1 quart	950 mL

WEIGHT

8 ounces	227 grams
10 ounces	284 grams
12 ounces	340 grams
16 ounces	454 grams

READ MORE

Besel, Jen. *Custom Confections: Delicious Desserts You Can Make and Enjoy.* North Mankato, Minn.: Capstone Young Readers, 2015.

Cook, Deanna F. *Baking Class: 50 Fun Recipes Kids Will Love to Bake.* North Adams, Mass.: Storey Publishing, 2017.

Eboch, M.M. *Foolproof Frozen Treats with a Side of Science.* North Mankato, Minn.: Capstone Press, 2019.

Huff, Lisa. *Kid Chef Bakes: The Kids Cookbook for Aspiring Bakers.* Berkeley, Calif.: Rockridge Press, 2017.

INTERNET SITES

Use FactHound to find Internet sites related to this book.

Visit *www.facthound.com*

Just type in 9781543530216 and go.

ABOUT THE AUTHOR

Heather Kim is a pastry chef, painter, and tattoo artist at Minneapolis Tattoo Shop, an all-female owned and operated parlor. Her deliciously unconventional desserts have been praised by the Minneapolis *Star Tribune*, *Minnesota Monthly*, and *Eater*. She lives in Minneapolis with her college sweetheart, Scottie, and their schnauzers, Max and Nietzsche.

Check out all the books in the Sassy Sweets series.

Compass Point Books are published by Capstone
1710 Roe Crest Drive, North Mankato, Minnesota 56003
www.mycapstone.com

Image Credits
Photographs by Capstone Studio: Karon Dubke, except:
Shutterstock: Arayabandit, 6 Bottom Left, atdr, 4 Bottom Left, Becky Starsmore, 7 Bottom Middle, ffolas, 14, Iakov Filimonov, 6 Top Right, Michal Schwarz, 4 Middle Left, photogal, 33, Sean van Tonder, 6 Bottom Right, VictorH11, 6 Top Left, W Photowork, 7 Bottom, wavebreakmedia, 4 Top Left, Yuliya Gontar, Design Element, 4–5, 46–47

Editorial Credits
Abby Colich, editor; Juliette Peters and Charmaine Whitman, designers; Tracy Cummins, media researcher; Karon Dubke, photographer; Sarah Schuette, photo stylist; Laura Manthe, production specialist

Library of Congress Cataloging-in-Publication Data
Names: Kim, Heather, 1978– author.
Title: Sweet and sour : far from ordinary fruity desserts / by Heather Kim.
Description: North Mankato, Minnesota : Compass Point Books, a Capstone imprint, [2019] | Series: Sassy sweets | Audience: Ages 9-11. | Audience: Grades 4 to 6.
Identifiers: LCCN 2018017830 |
 ISBN 9781543530216 (library binding) |
 ISBN 9781543530261 (ebook pdf)
Subjects: LCSH: Desserts—Juvenile literature. | LCGFT: Cookbooks.
Classification: LCC TX773 .K226 2019 | DDC 641.86—dc23
LC record available at https://lccn.loc.gov/2018017830

Printed in the United States of America.
PA021